IN THE SHADOW
OF AL-ANDALUS

ALSO AVAILABLE

BY VICTOR HERNÁNDEZ CRUZ

The Mountain in the Sea

Maraca

Panoramas

In the Shadow of Al-Andalus

POEMS

VICTOR HERNÁNDEZ CRUZ

COFFEE HOUSE PRESS
MINNEAPOLIS 2011

Coffee House Press books are available to the trade through our primary distributor, Consortium Book Sales & Distribution, www.cbsd.com or (800) 283-3572. For personal orders, catalogs, or other information, write to: info@coffeehousepress.org.

Coffee House Press is a nonprofit literary publishing house. Support from private foundations, corporate giving programs, government programs, and generous individuals helps make the publication of our books possible. We gratefully acknowledge their support in detail in the back of this book. To you and our many readers around the world, we send our thanks for your continuing support.

Good books are brewing at www.coffeehousepress.org

⌒⑭⌒

LIBRARY OF CONGRESS CATALOGING-IN-PUBLICATION DATA
Cruz, Victor Hernández.
In the shadow of al-andalus: poems / by Victor Hernández Cruz.
p. cm.
ISBN 978-1-56689-277-3 (alk. paper)
I. Title.

1 3 5 7 9 8 6 4 2
PRINTED IN THE UNITED STATES
FIRST EDITION | FIRST PRINTING

ACKNOWLEDGMENTS
Some of the poems in this book previously appeared
in *Black Renaissance Noire* and *A Gathering of the Tribes*.

031436403

To Amina Ouizzan
and our son Mohammed Amine of Morocco, North Africa,
who share in the blood and spirit of al-Andalus.

"In the end, much of Europe far beyond the Andalusian world, and far beyond modern Spain's geographical borders, was shaped by the deep-seated vision of complex and contradictory identities that was first elevated to an art form by the Andalusians."

—MARIA ROSA MENOCAL
The Ornament of the World

"When, later, Castile expanded southward the Arabic-Romance vernacular of Andalusia became the foundation of the Castilian tongue."

—ROBERT S. BRIFFAULT
The Troubadours

"Andalusia, because of the dynamism that comes to it due to its mixture of bloods and races, it is of such condition that it liberates itself from logic in favor, not of philosophy, which one supposes, but in favor of dream, of mystery and esotericism. Andalucía saves itself from the bondage to logic. . . . Andalucía is a province cultivated for surrealism . . . it is not saved from narrative even the musicians are narrators."

—FRANCISCO UMBRAL
Lorca Poeta Maldito

"I am the sun that shines in the sky of the sciences, My only defect is that my orient is in the occident."

—IBN HAZM
Córdoba poet (994–1064)

Introduction

Ay lelo layla, le lo lei.

This book has been a way for me to imagine history, Spanish and Caribbean. To untangle knots, layers of weaving. Many of these poems focus on the culture and society created during the middle ages in Spain.

I am in the shadow when I am in Morocco, which is right below Andalusia, and I am in that same shadow when in Puerto Rico, through language and culture. The Caribbean New World societies were founded in the same year, 1492, when the Christians reconquered Granada. The Taino societies of the Caribbean were invaded by a people that were still under the spell and influence of Muslim-Arabic culture. Moorish al-Andalus was an advancement in human society; at a time when European cities like Paris and London were in squalor, Muslims, Christians, and Jews, working in unison, lifted Córdoba to be one of the most thriving and progressive cities on the planet. The condition of women in al-Andalus was also much more advanced than in other parts of the world. Many women poets cultivated their poems, and both women and men touched upon erotic themes openly. No Islamic society has been this open ever since.

In Córdoba, there were well-paved streets lined with oil lampposts to facilitate night strolling, libraries, hospitals that treated all ailments, including facilities for mental health care. Arab scholars partook in the translation of Greek philosophical and scientific texts, creating a setting that reintroduced this material to the West. It is generally agreed that this impulse is what inspired the European Renaissance. There was a thriving ceramics and leather arts craft environment. The garment trade flourished, silk was introduced. The troubadour poets' influence took hold of Provençal and from there influenced the origins of European lyric poetry.

I have often traversed Andalusia on my way home to Morocco and back on my way home to the Caribbean. I have acquaintances there and have lived many adventures.

My poetry sits on the border of many languages. My first language of Spanish was interrupted when my family joined the migratory wave from Puerto Rico to New York City. I was five and my Spanish was intact, and I placed English grammar on top of my phonetic Spanish. To this day I have an accent in both my languages, as if I were not fully rounded out in either one. It makes for a slant and a twist in both my thoughts and word patterns that I have learned to cultivate, and as time passes I enjoy the cubist fragmentation. It is now a collision of languages, as I am surrounded by the Arabic of my family in Morocco and French is the second language there—much television and radio is in French and there are Arabic- and French-language newspapers.

Occasionally in these new poems I co-switch between Arabic and English as I once did between English and Spanish. Poetry moves with me to new geographies, languages, cultures, and religions. I speak with difficulty the local Moroccan dialect, which is known as Darija. It is a combination of Arabic and French, Berber, and Spanish words, because of the close proximity and the historical relationship with the Iberian Peninsula. For kitchen Moroccans just use *cocina*—in so many vocals I am right at home. And who could not make out *almuada* (pillow) from *almuad*? The Spanish language contains thousands of words derived from Arabic. It seems to me that I am in a tsunami or an earthquake of languages. Languages have collapsed all around me. Through it all I want to come out swimming toward the shores of expression, which is the purpose of poetry; giving words flavor, which is the highest poetic achievement, otherwise the words are all sleeping in the dictionary. I come from the contraband mountains of the Caribbean and not always are we in accord with the Real Academia Española. We have always been inventing a culture of necessity full of vigor and flavors, where all the races have jumped in the pot to cook a people's stew—such is the Caribbean. And such was the society created in al-Andalus by the Muslims: the Caribbean was the new Córdoba. Such is also the case of Morocco, the mestizaje so similar to my Puerto Rico, it makes me wonder where am I—should I speak Spanish or Arabic?

I do encourage you to look up the history of al-Andalus as you savor these poems. This is not a history book, for what I have done is imagined history—accuracy is for the encyclopedias. These poems are what historical realities have suggested to me. I am asking questions of history and have answered them through imagination. It is a way of expanding upon "identity." Our mother country is Spain, yes, but we must include North Africa as one of our maternal abodes as well. Our first contact with Africa came through the Muslim expansion into Andalusia; it included the Berber tribespeople (Amaziri) of the Almohads and the Almorivides. Our first contact with Arabic and Islam comes through the Spanish language. The Almorivides come from southern Morocco and even below that from the zones of Senegal and Mali, Ghana; as such they were also mulatto, racially mixed. Spain gained much culture, architecture, music, cuisine from this encounter. It is all part of the identity of modern Spaniards and by extension of our Latin American realities as well, especially the Caribbean, the region of the first European contacts, where the first cities, Santo Domingo and San Juan, were established; we are the beginning of America. So welcome all ye Saxophones, bienvenue, marhaba, be our guest, make yourselves at home and blow, immigrants.

To understand al-Andalus is to comprehend our modernity; the experiments they initiated continue here in our new world. I am within the influence of the Morisco troubadours, as we are under the Latino-Arabico-Afro-Taino sensibility throughout these islands. The troubadours also ignited modern European poetry. The Jews had a golden age in al-Andalus—the great philosopher Maimonides wrote his Jewish Hebrew intuitions in Arabic. Arabic was the lingua franca of commerce and scientific thought. Much of Spanish poetic meters are a direct accentual translation of the measurements of classical Arabic poetry, the basis of Galicia-Portuguese poetics and the romancero popular with the Spaniards all about. Arabic poetry influenced all Spanish literary forms, and by extension European forms as well, all through the splendor of al-Andalus. Latin America, we are within the memory of the Kingdom of Nazari, the last Muslim region of Spain, when Muhammed XI, also known as Boabdil, handed over the deeds of the city to King Ferdinand and Queen Isabella in 1492. Christopher Columbus was somewhere in the audience taking in all the ceremonies. Sometime after that Columbus was given an audience with the monarchs within the serenity and beauty of the Alhambra, and he was given his long-sought-after contract to embark on his voyages of exploration. Where did he show up with two Muslim captains leading some of the boats? To these tropics of our islands.

Enjoy this poetry and its inquiry into history.

Victor Hernández Cruz
Hay Salam, Sale, Morocco
December 15, 2010

Postscript

As I finished the above introduction, the shadow from Andalusia darkened into shades of tears at the passing of the great flamenco singer Enrique Morente. The news came through Radio Nacional de España, which is picked up here in Meghreb like a clear local station; the reverse is also true, as Moroccan music radio and calls to prayer are picked up all over the southern scoop of Andalusia. Another sign of our shared history, radio does not recognize borders, crosses at will with laud and guitar vibrations, the trembling voices, the eternal soccer games. Fanatics on both sides.

Enrique had a poet's heart. He dedicated many years to singing the poems of Lorca, Miguel Hernandez, Jorge Guillen, and many other word creators. He also sang to the cubism of Picasso, the painter from Malaga.

I heard much flamenco guitar and canto jondo writing the inspirations contained within this book, so this toast from the streets of Sale goes out to Enrique Morente, gracias mi hermano, may you rest in Gitano rhythms. You have left us your songs, which are perfume forever. Musk that sings in a flowered red shirt, a gold chain near your heart, your pinky gold with orange stone, the Cathedral seemingly bowing along with the wisp of your voice, an ancient reverberation that melts all languages.

—VHC

THE MEHDI POEMS

WEAVING THROUGH HISTORY:
GEOGRAPHY OF AROMA

North Africa

The boat like a floating almond
The constant wind flow between Algeciras
And Tangiers
Coast to coast sailors wrapped in djellebas,
A flavor in the nomad stream.
Are they drum songs with
Tinges of Mali, Senegal-shaped skulls
Mixed with unknowable Berber Asia,
Atlas Mountains black white girls.
Mosque visible from road Sevilla toward Cadiz.
Africa's top head *ras* hat
She pulls me body strong
There is prelude foreplay
Of stone known as Gibraltar,
Which once Tariq stepped upon,
Before entering the green diamond
Emerald southern peninsular coast,
Viva Algeciras.

In the Atlas Mountains blonde
African Laylas of Morocco
Light flesh yellow reddish or sets of
Deeper browns,
The southern tribes have more shadow
Kink skulls hair of wire nerves
Runs from bed to the mirrors

Reflecting a zillion Fatimas.
Yet I stare at the Cathedral of Cadiz
From Mohammed v Avenue frontal minaret
Allah is great, immense.
The black eyes multiply in Andalusia,
An extension of desire,
My lust of yellow Mediterraneans,
A body of water dancing mountains,
Is it earth mounds or moving seaward *carabelas,*
Melody of guitar wavering Spanish-
Arabic mesh,
What is it I ask, is the island shaking?
What are we speaking: Spanish?
Sitting upon this antiquity of Caribbean
Stone.
The distance has come to me,
North Africa my feet.
The fingertips upon the wires
Popular island Navidad.
Jesus is a star in the rhythms
Of the mountain *aguinaldos*
Flashing prophetic December,
Above the San Juan sky
Filled with polvo dust
that floated from North Africa:
the orgasms of the Sahara.

Sand

Sahara is the thought of my word,
it has been an infinite fire
stretching into the firmament meadows.
Does the sand continue into the sky?
We are less than what we thought.
Hungry scorpion, desert of your eyes,
laserbeam from the stars are
the clocks in the night sky.
How they arrange themselves between the
windows indicates that it is spring.
Imazighen are free men and women
children are the wind,
they have survived the Romans, the
Latin fish that came out of the sea as knifes.
Stay away from the square form of their
houses, stay streetless under sky, close the tents,
circular upon the sand,
cooking lamb within tagines.
In the dessert the horizon is our spice.
Berber girls are the most beautiful in Morocco,
necklaces of silver like curtains across their cheeks,
they move shoulders and bounce buttocks
like shaking jello through red Argan terrain.
She goats penetrated with old gods,
a henna of geometry,
which is too immense to decipher,

possessed with the ganawah rhythms.
That's why from a distance
I just count the sand pebbles
jumping with the metallic castanets
across the curvature of the dunes,
where the only flowers are the colorful
jellabas of the girls
waving as they are eaten by infinity.

The Dance of Blood

The cello of Pablo Casals has gone walking through
    an Antillean street
responding to the name of Sonia,
she steps upon the wires connected and crisscrossed
    with the Amazon,
sprinkled with a Berber hip, acquired when she was a guitar
swimming out of the laud,
soon after her black hair is inside the testicles
of brutal sailors of the age of exploration;
a piercing in the air, a desire so jasmine,
scent there by godly desire.
Perhaps one of her strings jumped a square-
shaped instrument made of camel hide,
which went lucid through the Niger River
of the Lumcumi,
when the sun was at such an angle her shadow
fell north onto the tiles of a Granada mosque,
which was about to become a church.

Paper Worm

Before you were
holding a tree sliced thin
between your fingers,
Your eye fixed on the ink,
at a party where the molecules were
moved by the sun,
moisture came dressed
with its thread of vapors,
the only dancer was sound.
Before biblios there
were the jugglers, the troubadours, rhythmic syllables
cutting veins with the strings of lauds, as
the bards were coming back from war.

Adobe Wind

Is it La Llorona that soars in the wind
through the window pressing
like a scratch on our moving bones
as we pass the Bou Regreg River
on the bridge that divides Rabat from Sale.
All around seated shadows clutching bags
full of almonds and dates, mint tea.

Already I think I am among the Navajo
in some Arizona valley
It is all the same clay flesh.

Geometry I once saw
upon a rug hanging in Tucson
as evening hugged us

Now we march under the brilliant star sky,
red stone monuments darkened as the
sky turns pink-orange around the edges.
We are stopped by a river,
we hear the shrill cries of the lady,
the same reverberation that fills the Sale, Morocco-
bound bus,
calling us somewhere,
somewhere else.

Dawn in the Tropical Zones

In the distance valleys and mountains,
waves on the horizons.
Some pockets of morning fog
a view as if the trees were smoking cigarettes,
the leaves still wet from the night kiss of moisture.
Morning radio talk shows
accompanied by the flavor of coffee.
Gracias, the sun peeps over
the mountains,
praising the original goats that first
ate coffee beans
and danced in excitement
for the curious shepherd
from Yemen upon African earth,
who wondered, "Allah, what is in
those beans?"
Beyond the valley, small towns
awaken.
The caffeine pencils
the mountains into paintings, and a
tropic flute rotates one more
butterfly day in our dreams.
Everything looks so unreal, and
it is all fake,
even if the coconut splits
and one hundred naked virgins

with gazelle eyes caress you
by a river.

Is it not all backwards, now
that we imagine what is not here,
that paradise is somewhere else,
beyond the panoramas of compost
moving for an instant through the
sky like a falcon,
gliding in motion
over the green salad,
green color coming to eat you,
under an all-blue sky,
green *cottoras*, Miro-like
tiny reinita birds.
The eventual composition will join the
compost in the guayaba valleys
of our Taino heaven,
destiny of rancid fruit,
spoiled papaya, revolving eternal
wasted bones and crazy coconuts,
all of us flapping our bat wings
toward the guayaba of destructive
paradise.
What is coming is at hand.

Touch . . .

It's here, do you not see . . .

Manhattan Transfer

to my son Vitin Ajani Cruz

Once I knew a city
that I now dream in another country.
The tall animals with windows
put us all to lowlife
feeling so helpless against the
weight of the cement.
No sooner was one apartment residence
when once again we were dragging boxes
downstairs with my uncles,
rum drinkers who sang boleros
at night on rooftops with the
background of Con Ed
pipes coughing smoke.
The Mediterranean in our octopus salad
soaked in olive oil, in
the red of the African beans
where indigenous calabash struggled
to stay afloat in a sea of red liquid.
The Spanish language took us to divorce
court,
while the English fought battles against us.
When I was there knifes flew out of the bricks,
while the remnants of the Arab laud
floated down marble stairs holding
hands with the poetry of the boleros.
Occasionally dinosaurs popped out of windows,

like some kind of phantasmagoric,
wondering if the day had turned to night
and if the stars had fallen into the East River,
or if it was going to rain blood.
Run home slam the door and the picture of
San Miguel and the glass of water above the
entrance falls upon your head.

The old men of Poland and Jews from
Russia
dragged through the streets adjacent to
Tompkins Square Park.
What English they spoke was
slanted, like a drunk on New Year's Eve.
When the mountains turned into
the Chrysler Building and the Empire State Building,
the highest ovals of unreachable mangoes
disappeared below a gray cool sky.
When the snow came to color ice on
the windows—
eight below zero outside
with the wind in addition—
"my God,"
my mother said, "maybe we should not
have come here."
I was nowhere to understand.
Took to walking the cold streets
starring at the brick texture
under the dim city sky,
windows of kaleidoscope walls
helping my crackling vocals chewing

in this new tongue, English,
erasing the old phonetics,
rooms full of Spanish fixtures.
Not allowing the English to invade
fully,
the accent is the laceration of the battle,
the price of rivalry.
The ability to look back and forward
to what was to what is and to what
isn't ever right or just slanted,
off, like geography shakes off the map.
Location: a simultaneity of places,
sounds, not feeling complete where
I nomad my bones, travels of joyful
uncertainty. I like the going.
more than the getting there,
motion is my home town,
yet memories of the city
are the recurrence of my dreams,
a fragrance, music, a song,
voices bring back the vision
urban reptiles, monsters of my youth
in the walls of brick cemented
in a past that dances in front
of me,
as the darkness is invaded by the sunlight
leaking through my eyelids,
the roar of Manhattan elevating
the old streets of my survival.

Civilians Suffer in Sadr City's
Daily Gun Battles

The *New York Times* so says,
April 21, 2008.
Amazing I am so surprised I had to repeat it to myself:
Civilians Suffer in Sadr City's Daily Gun Battles,
battles with guns, civilians suffer,
that's something that isn't anything else,
as when you say really, in Sadr City, guns blasting
molest civilians crossing the streets,
thus they suffer,
in danger zones where now we know
men and women can't even look out
the windows,
no school today, shut as they are
for people are in hazard, jeopardy
flying speeding bullets straight through
the air or zigzagging,
this is what the newspaper implies,
that human beings who are the civilians
are having a bad time,
civic beings painful in Sadr City as every day
guns are shot,
as they say in battles, menacing, hostile metallic
beans, string beans if not small carrots
on fire everywhere, not to mention tank artillery
or bombs from airplanes, which as for mathematics

is addition on the top of the heads of
the civilians who suffer in Sadr City's gun battles,
if it were just guns they would be suffering already,
and who has electricity for television
or *mas* more, even water to flush the toilet,
to administer even a shit, which is
included in war.
Central communal water faucets; pails
lined up helping civilians just to get rid of
of what was once food,
for what is shit but fermented food,
the chemical of its breakdown,
simple, we eat shit, like
Civilians Suffer in Sadr City's Daily Gun Battles
headlines in Manhattan newspaper,
as once in Puerto Rico the jíbaro measurement
device said "A quarter pound of shit weighs more
than 100 pounds of cafe."
The writers thought brilliant the idea
that civilians invented
the suffering, consequently they for sure
mentioned that militia fighters, that is the rebels
of the Sadr militia, that it was them who
fired into children, seven fell and four
suffered as unto death.
Poor children image one was bleeding
profusely from shot from a bullet that
hit his arm.
The reader paying over four dollars for a
simple cup of coffee in Starbucks, NYC
for coffee you see is now a luxury in

the States, sees this horror in the foam of
cappuccino, which after the bubbles drop
he/she notices that indeed he/she
has paid over four dollars for half a styrofoam
cup of coffee,
that one bubble that exploded into a thousand
pictures,
of men shooting children in this crime *not me*,
fighting now with more caffeine,
burning little fluffy puppies and cats
whatever even moves in the streets,
not just civilians suffer in Sadr City's
daily rain of bullets, but any rat in the way,
casual bird flight roasts midair
or arabesque building fascia or chance
pigeon birds or precise wing colors of butter
that flies into opportunity heat point in space
like *unico* in a million.
Sadr City Daily: *Citizens Suffer*.

It is all nowhere near the house of the Clintons
in Chappaqua upstate New York,
where they barbecue beef, drink Merlot;
later Hilary fingers through
room-size closet for red or dark purple
pant-suits for campaign speeches
that once supported the war
now reversed,
knowing well to follow where the money walks,
which has turned antiwar,
otherwise husband and wife would have been
quite content with the Iraq victory, which

they both desired.
A bullet shower weekly, monthly, yearly,
how come right there in capital Bagdad
the war feels like it's fresh, just started,
nearby the North 'Merican green zone
where things happen *not* fit to print,
Civilians Suffer in Sadr City's Daily Gun Battles,
what if the Bush daughters together the same
join the army to go fight terrorism in Iraq,
now that would be news. Would it fit?

What with all this chaos where would children play?
Where would teenage boys y girls find places to kiss?
Who walks their dogs with all these
yankee dogs loose playing cowboys with civilians,
in Bagdad barrio,
not that you won't get shot by a midwestern hillbilly
who got away from his porno films to spray a
shopping mall in some here at home base,
wait 'til the veterans get back and realize the
hurt upon people they've caused.
Battles, guns, Sadr City folks watching bullets fly.
Citizens of their own country, the culprits, bring this
chaos upon selves,
outsiders media shoves as if the military u.s. wasn't.
We are fighting Al-Quaeda not citizens
repelling invasion, convincing even themselves.
False words is all that fits, as they print
by night,
to cover the sky with their hands in the light
of the morning sun.

For the Far-Out Experimental Writer

From a metaphoric depth a bearded man,
tenements Manhattan lifts his head,
neighbors next door noise coming right
through, can't hear the
low Bach music from radio,
why the commotion, he was losing track of
his characters, memory trailing off with
incense identify myrrh, foot stomping,
was it a dance/just early evening.
His novel heady pomp of lofty concerns
is a see-through into reality,
into behavior, motives.
Curiosity wants to know what's going on,
they must keep it down for the eminence of prose.
He goes to hallway, knocks next door,
a woman opens the door,
apartment full of people, candles on the table,
Bible with other books,
a woman at the kitchen table doodling on a blank
paper,
a glass of water clear is next to her,
just one woman at door attends bearded matter,
behind her the ceremony proceeds,
woman at table starts to squirm,
hands scratching the surface,
she jumps up chair goes across room

her eyes jump out of sockets
her hands fly in circles over her head,
a horse with a headless man atop
galloped across room,
writer at door looking in,
what's going on he wants to know.
Woman says horse with rider no head
just come in,
agape bearded mouth open looks
forgets the reason why he knocked,
in the background he hears burps,
sees a woman touching and eating candle fire,
suddenly something entered her and slammed her
against the linoleum,
voices were speaking out of people,
he recognized some of the people from
the building but they all looked hazy with
glazed eyes,
questions were being asked
a man with a women's voice answered,
someone else saw a knife floating across the room,
he tried to rush to the door but was stopped,
my people are here a young girl said,
woman at door translates for the writer,
it was people from elsewhere and a different age,
an epoch gone through the blood of geographic
migrations.
Someone yelled the sun was coming out,
but outside a dark sky equipped with moon,
another city, somewhere castles, somewhere
tents in a vast dessert, a fire in the cool caverns

of sunken Caribbeans
from the centuries where everything was upside down,
the sun falls into the caves of Camuy
to hear the language of its limestone tongues.

Neighbors were touching fingers
jumping with electricity,
the woman who had been sitting
comes back to table, yells that there
are letters inside the glass of water
trying to form a sentence.
Another woman squirming sliding through the
floor like a snake,
the possessed were interviewed by the present.
A woman he recognized as the resident called
the group to prayer,
finally they focused on the man at the door,
they had not seen him.
The women softly translated,
asked him if he wanted to come sit,
but he was possessed with silence,
he never registered his complaint
and went back to his novel.
He was trying to alter the state of narrative prose
by using irregular time sequences,
he was known as el beatnik in the building,
he used some method called paste up
in which random prose parts came together.
Back at work he left his door wide open,
he heard footsteps come into his apartment,
each time he looked no one was there.

Listening to the Music of Arsenio
Rodriguez Is Moving Closer to Knowledge

The sight of shadows dancing son montuno,
guaguancó darkness, all was black when fingers
had the fine memory of place, where they were
upon the strings of the streets
in the Spanish Harlem days of the great Cuban
tres guitar musician.

The Congolese arrived fully in the skin tightened
by wood,
came from the center of the continent,
where candles guided the fingers
in specific codes of ritual
opening like keys to dwellings of power
significant traditional authority,
a classical music of the rhythms,
it was boat travel between the realms,
New Yorker's eyes in awe, club Palladium
Broadway
erased the cement and bricks
saw lions and tigers coming toward them
rhinoceros and zebras dancing.
This blind man staring through his glasses into the forest,
it was eternal night, sometimes fire turned into
emerald and he saw a beat dressed as a suit,

a woman, her red dress made of achiote seeds
that escaped from maracas.

We listened to music hormone adolescence,
when the features of our masks were forming
from distant mangroves,
mestizos of Cubist fragmentation,
Carabali molasses with Amazonia wrists,
muñeca bone,
a Roman flare for sauces crocheted with
Castile olive oil, que viva Shango upon
the plantains.

The researchers will come to encounter
the puddles of water,
they will hear our voices and the shuffle
of feet,
wet all over the room of the loud Victrola.

Water for everybody, water destroying
everything, landscape geometry of structures.
How well did it clean? Everything is somewhere
else, swimming in that lake river sea.
We don't know if the Rio Grande flows toward the coast.
Lake Conga drum, the Guadalquivir listening to
the breezes of tres guitar evocative of Indian sitar
of Arabic laud sailing through the pomp vamp
of Cuban rhythm.

The flowers we see through the open curtain,
whistle in the afternoon, the layla lo lay of mountain songs,
nighttime.

The investigators finally ask:
"Where is everybody?
Are the windows opened?
Has it rained?"

●

You can get involved with a dot
'til it swallows your entire mind
hands and feet and ras   *(as to head somewhere else with it)*
if you cinematic roll,
you mess dot, 'til dot is all,
comes sits at the exit of what you
think is thought   *(at last inquiry self con self, mumbo mambo)*
a dot softly sits 'til it becomes bigger,
massages your eyeballs of perfect illusions.
A junkie can mess with a dot
or empty bottles of orange soda,
they zoom in with the camera,
come real close the body dangling
toward floor, standing or sitting, snap
out of it, before they fall as if they had springs.
          (a movie I saw dreaming I was in it)

Between the eye opened and the lids closed
you start to work that dot,
you think it's a mouth,
you see it move, do it have feet,
what dot doing there *(California delusion)*
We get convinced that the dot is a speaker
and we hear Dizzy Gillespie's "Manteca,"
you realize the lard of junk between your knees,
where is the dot below you or above?

(the first thing about conspiracy theories they are not there
the government wishes, they are the dope dealers)

One thing though, junkies got labial,
a form of rap consistent with skin rushes,
they have convinced Nuns to smush in hallways,
salesmen of leather coats in the summer
should send them overseas as ambassadors.
Don't ever give junkies brooms, they will
sweep all day into the night, then
wait for the sun to inspect for more debris.
If they find dot they walk inside
and scrape the borders of the circle,
scratch their legs with more uh blah ba lah.
    (bright sugar comes out of the mouth, chemical society—
    available for you to pay the bills)

Mescaline deep wonder.
Could it be your iris reproducing
outside of your eye?
And thus questions of Philo's
Logos come to your mind,
like Tata Güines slapping skull de vos,
    (another form of you taken for ride)
circle red timba that that dot sends
mothers into secret ether
and you will take years to clean dot
with rags and chemicals, thinking for
instance that cocaine is a plant,
eaten by the colorful hats the Incas wear,
forgetting or never data that it is an alkaloid

mixture of who knows what gasses, Ajax
flakes of contaminated bone,
snow of the Andes
such Quechua language
vocals   (*the sight of Puerto Rico melted the errors into memory*)

Now in bright sun
real magical clarity no longer see dots,
long gone, the earth a woman naked before me,
eating each other whole,
the tongue speaks exactly
the details of what it licks
        (*al Megrib-ability to see the star-Morocco*)
In the sky walking home,
the camel trots.

Abu Bakr Muhammad ibn al-Arabi

I walk now pages of your dance thought,
Murcia in your heart, city founded by Muslims,
epoch of turbulence in which you lived
but somehow peace came upon you in Mursiya.
The night from the hills, pictures the Bay of Cartagena.
Young, you left for Seville, it was a different
place. You left speaking many languages,
opening in your young mind the paths
toward Allah, as much knowledge/sense of paradise
as can be achieved upon the earth.
In Córdoba you met Ibn Rushd Averroes, the philosopher.
An epoch later you witnessed his funeral procession,
how a donkey carried his papers.
Contemplate how people are always at
different levels no matter who and in what
where or year of humanity, always the same
proportions. The clouds are pages
before the wind of the full text descends,
from darkness where knowledge lives.
Levels, proportions.
Jesus came to hold your hands,
marched with you to the Gates of
Paradise, it is not the same Isa that people
now church for.
Among the Christians, church is a form of entertainment,
you sit and listen to speech, or observe ritual.

Among Catholics, the priest alone partakes
in ritual, one sits like in a play, while the evangelicals
have descended to what the masses comprehend,
struggle out of hard harsh life. But you were the silence of
    the ascetics
in this lack of self before Islam, before religion,
the instinct of God nature.
The bodies take the worst option.
Pastor in front of congregation
"Yes, I was a drug addict, stooped down
so low that I stole from my own mother,
hallelujah, but Jesus came to the depths
of my streets and took me by the hand,
I saw the light, hallelujah, I saw the light,
illuminated my life, now I am in front of you.
ten years I don't do any drugs, hallelujah,"
the people repeat with him. The masses
are cured with this confession.

Islam differs in that one goes to mosque
and participates in a ritual, it is an
encounter with Allah, it is a body motion,
a routine to put you in celestial orbit,
in pursuit of the stations of the sun.
Ibn Arabi was not just religious
in orthodox light,
he had Christian and Jewish elements,
Greek philosophy. His father sent
him to meet the philos Ibn Rushd (Averroes)
in Córdoba. He was still a young man,
"beardless" as he himself has commented.

That such an encounter in such a
a Córdoba took place highlights the
knowledge of the times, of the ambience.
Where is Ibn Arabi writing right now?
Surely he is here somewhere.
He met people who were not of his
time, because life is outside of specific
place, moments. The man desired a young
ninfa girl, which is also a thirst of knowledge,
it is beauty, yes, it is also a sign
upon a path, it is an arrow pointing
in the direction you are going.
Gorgeous bonbon of ardent stare,
flames in the eyes, without thought
or program, we have learned
something. Awareness on its own
crosses the street,
where are we when we are,
who it it is that is here.
Arabi where are you,
are you with me,
walking toward the Centro plaza,
shapes and forms everywhere.
Are you with me in the mountains
of Luquillo,
when suddenly her eyes
arrow you together us, they can stop an elephant
in trot, but it is just my imagination.
Dream asleep.
Images of a new day erase her forms.
Insects I've never seen before,

light around large animals.
Where are the horses and the holy sheep?
The goats are entering pipes.
It is the sound lifting images
Averroes encountered during inspired
meetings with prophets, like Adam
explaining the original names of things,
the nature of his bones, *adam* creation.
Ibn Arabi told the great philosopher
that both positions lead to the same thing,
the scriptures recited and the fire of thought,
heart and mind,
poetry and philosofafa.
Jesus of Maria, heart of my mother's
invocation.
Moses, my hands, what do they
hold? Stroll with him into the
square, which you circle.
Was it thought that I dreamt or
dream that I thought?
it was a sleeping night wind.
The nomads do not understand.
Once upon a time I lived among them.
Not happy, they wondered if I had truly
achieved the religion,
because in
obedience, repetitive routine,
always like dogs open mouth.
Dreams are my Allah messages,
and when every day outside makes conflicts,
I sleep them away.

Awake in Fez, I travel with friends.
Before that I walked the beach of Tarifa,
where the Mediterranean Sea kisses
the Atlantic. What divides there, rivers
deposit sweet water, right hand, left hand,
clap.
The Sierras de Ronda lifting high,
the morning, the night, turning
body lands in ambience of Baghdad.
On to Maghreb. Fez,
so beautiful everything seen in
a kind of bluish light from the
afternoon sky.
Orange trees sweetness and fragrance.
I go with the camels whence they march,
the love of her eyes whence they beg,
the truth of this lie,
I offense into the night.
So much wind,
full moon, stars dance.
I am in Damascus, city of old bones
ragil cheriff.
The tongue still waters in my mouth,
for ninfas, delicious,
rising rising rise ballerinas.
I feel ascension toward
other paradises.
I still recognize so many things:
birds fly over a river,
gazelles sway to music,
pipes and drums,

charm of my son, the hands of my father,
sweet laugh daughter,
relations. A woman prepares mint tea
turning pages,
towering ears hear a wind shift.
Wait where is the bed, the mattress,
the softness of my almuad, my pillow.
I met them all through the thirst
of my desire. Camels came close
to us, didn't know if they were seeing us.
Who did I meet. All I know, later;
I found aroma like floating words
spread out through the sheets of my
thoughts. On certain days it was keys,
I search for the rooms, opening one
door after another, there is
nothing but endless doors.
The mineral stones, first in sight,
soft green foliage reaching for light
water forever for everything.
An orange fish for Jesus comes
forward to kiss me,
Maimonides sings to me in Hebrew,
Ibn Rushd is smiling as if into the
nature of phonetic people.
What brings us here on wings of sound.

This joy to how many streets has it come,
it repeats through eternal awakenings.
How can we comprehend the birds
in our hands,

if others see cashews, pecans and almonds,
brown sugar?
Someone holds my hands as everything
greens.
She kisses me. Welcome, Malhaba
to some realm of infinity,
gardens of books,
rows of flowers,
black and white raisins.
Sweet to touch the flesh
of the air
as I awake from my dream.

Mexico City

to Ishmael Reed

Ah to be with the dead
with the circle bone moon
like an eye of a seed that gave fertility a
vibrant color that decays in the murderous air,
stone barren, dreaming when her lips were red wet
dispensing an endorphin like a rain of desire.
In the Zocalo Plaza the sound of crackling skeletons
in the night of November dos,
crossing the flowers growing out of skulls,
what guayaba beauty that houses with
bats flying toward the sickness the festering
sweet fruit. Sugar, the jungle whispering in the city.

Tiyanquiztli marketplace of chocolate and vanilla
baking and eating skull cookies, frijoles with
my eye tacos, frijol enchiladas
Tenochtitlan upon the lake a canoe
passing floating flowers,
to flash that only the exterior was conquered,
the inside Mexica feather wind continues.
Original time, Ollin the movement click,
the doctors that divided the eye into its parts,
to look at the Astros pacing its celestial movement,
measure in the zero, 365 days clear.
Where was the world when Montezuma, in his

palace of one hundred rooms
each with a bath of jade,
walked out to the botanical gardens
gulping fried iguana with chilies?

Twice in the D.F. first time huge hotel on Avenida
        Reforma
during the big quake, I read years later that the very
        hotel where
we stayed, crumbled like an implosion, temblors can be
        any instant,
we are always one breath away from passage.
Look, the marble, first-floor lobby,
I can see through the bamboo of the years,
so many birds flew toward the sun
looking for boas curving through the fires to eat them.

Last day of conference, with the writers' ideology
tossing, corners of polemics,
Ishmael and I decide to go see the pyramids of
Tenochtitlan, the moon and the sun
and Nezahualcoyotl reclined like a state poet
in an art deco seat.
We foot the bone steps of pyramid earth.
At the top of the sun I look down
to spot Ishmael and his big Olmec chocolate head
staring into the prose of eternal stone.

The warriors eating the silky slight bush
of Guadalupe,
part Arabic, part Latin.

Her new name in her old space.
Walking through the drums in sandals,
the clock of the feathered maracas,
knees lifting toward Venus,
the tribe like Egyptians in space suits.

Second time in District Federal
from the plane way above shrub-covered mountains.
Where's this continent city?
Awe puzzling streets of endless lines.
Mounds of gray rock.
When we finally fell into the valley,
it looked like the inside of a portable radio
stretched out like an ocean,
opened up to that panel of cables, wires,
little round and oval silver objects with copper wiring.
What is all this, the whole horizon dotted with
something, the whole basin occupied,
the airplane motion forward, perhaps not the city.
Forty minutes later, the captain announces our descent into
the eternal urban jungle, the end of the world.
Small hotel, sleeping the night, a caravan, the street
eight floors below. I peered through the window.
Military trucks roaming the districts to check everything,
maintain military fear.

Morning going down elevator
it was like a vertical coffin with rugs for walls
a dust gray, dim lightbulb, a sluggish speed.
Once I get out of this I'll never
. . . the stairs.

Saw then where last hotel
stood, a crater.
So many buildings gone, replaced by worse,
part of the metropolis lost.
Gone the Mayan philosophers, out of view
of the conquest,
leaving enough city to still be the biggest upon
Earth. The beginning and the end of cities.
Flower and song that decays in the evening
with the sinking sun.

We disappeared back to strange
Northern California, Bay Area,
contemplate, so much new language
sifting through the ruins of antique
stone, with tecolote owls stationed
by candles, one chocolate letter
waking another, the poem is on its own
bone,
skeletons of cookies dancing the
Mission District rumba,
all of us crumbling back toward
flesh light.

Dolores Street

for my daughter Kairi

We lived in an old Victorian building
round the corner from Dolores Park,
it was a corner building,
A window ledge the place
I sat to study esoterica of gone races,
concealed historians, scholarship of mist
covering chaos.
Thoughts that terrified me about the human,
Gazing below onto 18th Street.
Up a ways on Dolores Street was the
Old Mission Dolores Iglesia, the first
Christian Spanish church in the city,
buried there were Iberian
bones along with native bones, it was the
northernmost border of Mexico, it was
native tongues and Castillian language
suspended there for generations of their
syllables.

It was the year when I stood home taking
care of my daughter, while she slept I read
books on the occult, Gurdjieff, tarot cards,
Augustus Le Plongeon and his Mayan-quiche,
Egyptian-Atlantis and Indian Kundalini connections.
The sphere of Orion, chambers lost in
primordial brain vanished wisdom in the
frijoles of my tacos.

I gave thought cannabis to a crystal city
arising off the waters of the Haiti of my Caribbean
Sea.
Studies had me possessed walking the Mission
streets thinking I was in Palenque, in the Guatemala
confines of mind, burning tortillas on the stove,
we were all natives banished from our own
nativity.

I took my daughter to Dolores Park,
played on the swings, walked on the mounds
of green grass, we had an elevated view of
downtown, the new pyramid building, beyond,
we actually saw Bahia water with
a glimpse of the Bay Bridge.

Flash of the early euro united statesmen
roughnecks, gamblers and chewers of
tobacco with whisky, low culture cattle muck
kerosene lamps, wooden planks leading
to doorways of malfunction homes,
small vocabularies full of elongated passions.
This San Francisco dock of the bay,
the end of the earth. The collected debris
that came west on Interstate 10 and took
the old roads north to this region of hills
finding here a Spanish enclave,
which they plastered with houses, wood, some cement.
It was all mountains, hills, which they forced
to inhabit city life but still
going up these streets you feel the car will flip over,
the mountain street end wheels up.

It was years of this exile that my son and daughter
grew,
cold damp apartment like Mark Twain knew,
it's an implosion chill takes your bones out
walks them to the freezer leaves them there overnight.

It wasn't me there but something like a plant
drinking water
learning to reach into the
sun of the books by window shelves
nourishment for future language,
Mission High School just one block away,
I am distracted from la poesi by the big radio
of teenagers going toward the park,
couples boys and girls,
finally the silence of time counting
itself, waves of space later
I hear Malo's Suavecito radio coming again,
the kids going back home holding hands
clothes wrinkled eyes like red clouds.

That same day my daughter hid inside a
closet veiled by a curtain, went missing.
The windows were all open. I looked out
each one, I went down the back stairs,
asked the neighbors,
frustrated about to cry,
I had become an animal searching for
its offspring,
when I heard a giggle, pushed the curtain open,
there she was.

She had been playing a game on me,
my nerves gave her three whacks.
It was all in that corner of my past,
which floats in the currency
of the river like a bubble
before it bursts against the sharp
reality of her new drawings and
colors, which she always becomes
for me.

Clan

to my cousin Hugo Velazquez

What can I tell you about my family,
that they were immense gulps of desire,
melancholic secret rivers of tears, struggling peoples
thrown onto a scenery that had nothing
to do with them?
At the height of young life a collision
with a new language,
the signs were indecipherable,
windows floating high, bricks in between.
Within that assault, derailment from
the tropics, a leap in time and dimension,
a jump upon the cubist canvas
fragmentation of our reality,
within chaos
decisions had to be made.
Our sexual bodies spilling into action,
where are we?
The children of such broken particles,
angry discussions of night,
we take bread out of the oven either uncooked
or on fire,
like César Vallejo said *a bread burnt at*
the door of the oven,
burnt on a day that God was sick, but we took
it and many of us survived, grateful
sons of malcreations.

When you follow it,
when you are strongest those young years
is when you mistake the bad for the good
and have no way of seeing it different.
Relatives showed up.
They also had jumped like frogs
and landed in Manhattan
on the third floor of the cold water railroad
flat, Lower East Side, where we lived
talking about Korea, some of my uncles,
Army uniforms, shining black shoes.
Another uncle showed up with a German wife,
a small baby in her arms,
he had been military stationed somewhere
Berlin.
My mother saw it
said take the baby to the doctor, it's going to die,
and it was at Bellevue Hospital where it
happened next day when they took the little creature,
his mestizo features inside white skin.

Some relative of a cousin, family branch
in deepest Brooklyn, had the name Guatengo,
strange sound to me, I ask him what doing
in New York with a name like that. Back on the island
they specialize in naming people, based on
looks or something they have done, he looked
like he just popped out of the Amazon jungle,
we watched him those first days off the boat
dazed by the English, years passed, when saw him
again he's talking English and wearing a gold

watch and he's going to see Murray the K's
Paramount Theater soul and rock & roll presentations.

My aunt Carmen had hallucinations, always
some half dream, she said that my
grandmother's picture shook on the wall across
from her bed 'til her mother came out of the picture
and appeared life-size in front of her.

Older story still in island town, my mother
had some uncle they called Chivato,
he was a carpenter, an electrician, he made
coffins, painted them with images of fruits and
flowers,
he moonlighted as some kind of doctor
crackling neck bones.

His wife did things by rivers
in the dark of night,
worked with lizards and people's names
written on paper. She stuffed them inside
frog stomachs, worked with ammonia,
chicken blood, full moon better,
always an owl nearby tree. No one
ever looked into her eyes.

This surrealism all before migration,
little town talking Spanish,
Meyo invented a circus with a group of friends,
put up curtains in an empty lot,
had a series of acts, a man who tied lizards

and made them dance, that's what he said,
could have been the minireptiles just
getting away. Meyo himself got dressed as
a woman and jumped into the audience
rubbing his fake tits in the faces of the men
who turned red. They had a puppet show,
the puppets recited poetry.
Classical Spanish.

My grandmother took my mother to work
with her splicing tobacco leafs in half
despalillar is what they called it.
What they paid: it was a form of slavery.
The women brought the leafs down to the
chinchals, tobacco workshops stacks
of brown moist tobacco leafs folded
inside burlap sacks
balanced on their heads walking
the five blocks to the shops
where the men drank brandy and black café
as they rolled.

Relative of my father was a horse trainer,
had a horseshoe-nailing stand in the
principal street, this the 1930s. One day when four
horses were waiting, one drifted down the
street unnoticed, as the men were
drinking rum from the earth,
that illegal stuff they call *pitorro*.
Happens this door was wide open,
the horse stuck its long neck in and

saw himself in a mirror on a wall,
horse saw its own image, and the
caballo thought it was a mare and charged
the mirror, went through the wooden wall into
the neighbor's bedroom where the animal
saw himself again in a mirror he kept
charging after himself 'til he knew not where
he was, or what he was doing.
He lost his way out and kept running through
rooms, this is the alley of a poor barrio,
people saw that beast, they were screaming and jumping
out of windows like they seen the devil. Finally
the horse found an alley that led to the main
street down from the horseshoe place.
The men went after him, caught up with the horse,
mouth foaming mucus and saliva middle of the
public plaza, didn't want nobody to go near
it, not even the owner, police show up, owner
asks one of them for the big Colt .45,
goes up to the mad horse, shoots it
point blank between the eyes, twice,
the beast collapsed, everybody's
eyes popped out of their sockets. Back in the
alley the neighborhood people talking that
the horse finished the district, more than
twelve houses damaged, no one slept that
night, some said that the horse was possessed
with some demon. Next day fixing the damage,
neighbors threw rose water, Agua Florida, and blew
cigar smoke into everything.

We used to jump down a ravine just at
the edge of town, at the bottom of the river
where the women went to wash clothes
my grandmother and mother among them,
together they slapped and pounded clothes
against clean rocks.
Nearby there were cows, sometimes goats,
my grandmother always with a head scarf,
the children, in such pristine lush,
climbed trees, and with a large strong
vine we swung ourselves into the river, a spot that
was about six feet deep.
Abuela sometimes called me over
to get closer to her and my mother,
but children just want to play.
Now a grown adult, I go by that spot
and it all looks so diminished, so small,
the river is but a stream subtracted from the immensity
I once sensed.

Into this future I see my
grandmother and mother bright
in the thick of black dream night.
My people always come while
I sleep, I see vivid the past,
even family I never saw,
people who were old when my mother
was young. If I saw them it was brief and
swift from the corner of my eyes.

Cica, my mother's aunt
Augustina's sister,

lived in a native bohio.
When my mother was about ten or eleven, there were
still native huts in the mountain Jagueyes,
she'd go there with her mother, whose skin
was color of tobacco leaf. The huts were round or like
a pentagon, hammock to swing in just outside,
the floor was compressed dirt, it was 1937,
no electricity, at night the kerosene lamp
known as *quinque*, outside the area of the
fogon cooking with wood center upon rocks,
elders say everything tasted better back then.
I met Cica when I came to Puerto Rico in 1989,
she was puzzled by the modern people, truly
she was a child of the turn of the century,
I couldn't even explain to her this
thing called writing. For her, poetry was
breath in the air, the songs of the troubadours,
guitars like the minstrels who pushed up
from Andalusia to the courts of Provençal,
'til the tongue licked ink upon paper.
She left to her now cement house
before dark, before the duendes flew
through night, before La Llorona
beckoned from the rivers.

Carlos, my mother's brother,
arrived in New York after serving U.S. Marine
time in Korea, that was the crown of
his life, he'd always sing that Marine song
"from the shores of Tripoli . . ." he knew little English.
When he spoke to English speakers he tried

to make pictures with his hands.
Lower East Side circa 1959, he wandered
around the corner where there was a bar,
drank and conversed with other men,
got dulzon tipsy like caramel melt,
when he got out, wanted to get back.
What inferno carajo, the building where is it?
Forgot even how he got there,
a taxi was coming down the street,
the address of our building he had written on a
piece of paper, he showed it to the
the driver who knew it was just
around the corner yet he took him
off for a ride, took the FDR Drive,
exit on Houston Street and came back up
Avenue C, Carlos his eyes half closed,
woke up when they turned the corner
onto our block. It was two dollars,
some money for that period.
Two days later my uncle wanted to hit
that same bar again, a friend told him
"come on let's go," he walked him around the
corner, and that's when he knew that he had
been taken, he told his friend "there's
lots of sons of whores here."

In the green world before we jumped on the
propeller plane for the gray cement sky world, in
my father's family, no one could read,
not my Grandma Alejandrina.
Not my grandfather, who only saw me

twice, disappeared into the vines
of his agricultural indifference, up there
with insects undiscovered unregistered.
Mountains created individuals
with no sense of anyone or thing other than
themselves, they were people of recitation
and numbers, my father's tribe all fingered
money, were good with ciphers, without thought,
my mother's
side the opposite, all her brothers showered
with rum within the bohemian strolls of the bolero,
womanized, kept no track of legitimacy.
My own father called them leather
"might as well burn your money or throw it away.
They will leave you as peeled as a chicken's ass."
Natalio, my father's uncle, was like radar with money,
but couldn't read one letter. If he looked
at print, he saw it as shapes or designs,
and yet he had a little grocery known as Colmado
and he made there what everybody wanted—
dinero, plata. MONEY.
He traveled in jitney van busses
through the regions that surround Aguas Buenas,
Cidra, Comerio, Bayamon, looking for
wholesale deals for his grocery,
came back the same day with shopping
bags, or burlap sacks,
no one would ever beat him out of a penny.
He once spotted a quarter shinning down
a ravine, it called him right through
the foliage,

curvy terrain, slants, rocks, he dove after the
coin and deduced that whatever
he bought in town was twenty-five cents cheaper.
They always measured that way.
This class can wait too.
One time a man was going to sell him ten chickens
at a price that was like buying seven, three would
be like free.
Natalio that morning lifted his head off his pillow at 4:00 a.m.,
could not sleep, insomnia of the profit margin.
Went to the stop designated for the reunion
in the hot valley of Caguas—the June sun
poured fire toasting the region near the
old chimney of an extinct sugar central.
Natalio waited and waited while
the chicken farmer's pickup was broken down
curving up some isolation out of Aibonito
near some urugutoon two miles away
where the chicken vender had to walk to
to get a mechanic.
He passed five hours waiting,
almost passing out under the sun with
no tree shadow to nail down,
three hours into it he walked to a cafetin
he was going to buy a Kola Champaign
but found the price two cents over what
he sold it for at his place and just asked
for an empty box, cardboard to cover the sun
walked back and umbrellaed himself
another couple of hours 'til the chicken
man arrived.

When the man arrived neither of them
said a word about their ordeals
went right to business, my dad's
uncle saw the chicken back of pickup,
jumped in front and headed back to town
for the trackqueteo.
Any modern person would
have collapse.

Who was my grandfather's father,
and what of his grandfather?
Are they in my dancing shoes?
How many generations do
we have to go back
before we come upon a different language
or elevate with a guaraguo falcon flying above
the snake curves of a river,
hear the native names of the trees,
Maria is that still you,
darker copper dance breeze.
Never mind about so far back,
I never knew my father's father
and I was an adult when his last breath
was taken back by Dios.
So many links back, get back to the ships,
sail back to Andalusia, and who knows who came
from where, Sevilla or Córdoba, Granada,
or Málaga, mas Ronda. . . .
Was it home to this fragment of the tapestry
or more at Jerez de la Frontera near the
mountains covered with olive trees?

When they came to mix with the jaguar claws
of the Amazona,
and the shadow eyes of mucaros,
Caribbean owls,
bone deep within resides the African tulip trees
blanketing mountains with red flowers,
the coast kept moving inland
away from the boorish pork chops.
Enjoy this cocktail,
because if history does reverse, we descend
descend, unraveling from variety, the blood
will become closer and closer 'til we march
ourselves into a province
where cousin marries cousin, collapse
down precipice into Bronze antiquity caves,
knocking on the gates of paradise,
the first family—Adam preferred Eve
and couldn't womanize none,
as all the other females were his daughters.
That's the rhythm of a Middle Eastern religion,
the Bible's Christian words,
a beat where desire descended through sight,
the sky, penetrated Maria through her eyes
fertilizing through the center of the pupils.
Everything came from Silence,
Popul Vuh recollecting that calm space,
It was the dance floor before the band arrived.
Movement stirs out of nothing,
nothing is nothing,
creation is something out of nothing,
could there be anything less than nothing,

desire is the initial movement, charge of energy,
sliver of light cutting air to will something out of
nothing.
Willy.
As the first peoples original Caribbeans say
all water was once inside a calabash gourd,
a higuera oval hanging from which they also made
maracas,
lizards put foot atop rocks earliest and with
reptilian vision, noticed the first flower.

My Uncle Samuel, father's brother,
came to New York with borrowed suit,
everything he owned on his back,
gathered money as that tribe is attracted
to cash, truly it comes to them,
saved until he mounted a bodega, 9th and D
across the street from the Jacob Riis Housing Projects
late fifties–early sixties, them projects right there
swarming with Caribbean mouths—
those buildings were like beehives,
all those mouths hungry in bilingual.
Police had a habit of shaking
bodegas down because of a city ordinance
you couldn't sell beer on Sundays,
no one paid it any mind, just gave the local
"blues" a twenty along with a couple of beers,
which they quickly drank in the back
sitting upon sacks of Rosita beans.
Two Irish cops came to my uncle's store
looking for their allotment,

but Samuel was in a different mood,
asked them to go away,
not today.
They stayed and insisted,
'til they saw no go.
They told him to close and go home,
inside my uncle asking
who were those two pink beefsteaks
trying to ruin my day.
One of them close to the counter pulled out
his revolver.
Samuel quick like a shoe along with step
puts a hatchet—razor-sharp tool for cut meat—
right on the neck, right on the jugular.
"You shoot and I fall on your neck
and hack you head to pieces."
The other cop hand on gun,
frozen statues in front of him.
Some kid opened the door, saw the
plastic art and backed out without
the pound of Café Bustelo he was sent to get.
The cops backed down, it wasn't the
kind of day they had planned.
Samuel we see you next Sunday,
not knowing that the bodeguero
was schizophrenic beyond recall.
In New York all Samuel wanna
do was fight police.

Gaspar and Augustine, family of grandmother,
maternal side,

supplied African genes dancing with the mix of
rice and beans,
bouncing throughout the nineteenth-century
small towns,
working odd jobs to survive the
hard times after Spanish-American War,
a small store where they sold
what the mountains produced.
Had they just come from somewhere coast,
brought to work in the Caguas Central sugar,
did they still have the marks where they were
branded as owned meat by the Castilian
iron fire? *Carimbó*
Escaped Cimarron's native huts,
left his daughter Cica in the bohío my mother
visited as a child.
I am with them in the night enclave,
Aguas Buenas still a barrio of Caguas
over the mountain.
When they dropped down into the town—
four streets—they shared a room.
Round from the plaza were parked
horse-driven carts—same place today
carro publicos, gasoline epoch.
Augustine in love with my grandmother's mother,
shadows kissing under flamboyant trees, mangos
falling onto their kisses sweetly.
I look with him through the crevices
of the wooden walls, old house quinque lamp shadows,
we see big dragon ox whipped by
pieces of cane. He can smell the cargo of

carbon and yautia and panas going toward
the main street stores, coguis singing their mating call
all night, celebrating reptile vagina, later
the silence of the daylight coitus.
All those people were born up
in that mountain, Jagueyes, my grandmother,
her sister Cica, the brothers, some more I
don't know, that fertility rolled down
into town like fog.
Do I see him like a shadow within a landscape
figure with machete down the curve of Lorca green?
Andaluz *verde que de quiero verde.*
As I read the investigative letters of slavery
and feudalism, the snobbish landowners
who ate every young india and mulata
that moved upon their land,
my hands get goose pimples.
Praise hands that labor.

Ñeco, he was part human
half rooster, somewhat horse, calabasa,
eyes of falcon guaraguo.
He was a relative my father's side.
He was a gallero, trained roosters to fight,
sport, like beak boxing. He also worked for
a local farmer, taking malanga, yautia,
chayote, ajies through island pueblos,
knew the whole date oval 110 by 36
square mile country though this does not include
the caves and the sky and the kisses that
define the mileage of the heart.

I sat with him before he went
circa 1985. He talked about roosters and plants,
vegetables and women and jealousy, about
the truck
he had 1966 in the town of Arecibo
up on the coast north,
in the countryside, how he ran out of gasoline,
had to walk into town,
and the ordeal turned into a memory of
the beautiful women he saw there on
the way to the centro to get some help.
If you want to see women, he said,
I mean *women*, go to Arecibo.
So I left the next day,
walked through all its streets
many of which fell into the sea,
and saw the sirens that floated
in water blue languor
a reflection of the sky, mouth open
like I heard a song
I was in Lena Horn heaven
that afternoon, which is now, the camera,
the pictures of black eyes, curvy spilling
hazelnut aroma.

The hidden place of my mother,
an insecure universe,
fearful somewhere deeper inside,
a courage that would rage
in the interior that opens, exactly
dedication of her motherhood.

The Hernández tribe had these slashing tongues,
words that pierce.
they could hurt you with sound,
filtered through passion
not through thought.
We are in New York.
The airplane big bird, took almost nine hours,
Pan Am, her hands always tending me,
finally in the tenement flat
she threw me in the kitchen sink washing me
same Octagon soap she did the clothes with.
I breastfed a long time,
maybe 'til almost three,
Italian peasant style.
In the small Rican town she had to start helping abuela and
five brothers, clean house, wash clothes, cook . . .
She married a force of wind taking her
to the altar,
that whole social class in the hands of custom
faith, the wheel of repetition.
Balcony the evening sitting around singing
my grandfather, guitar and mountain troubadour,
that Hernández tribe, they all sang,
my mother was the life of the boleros,
in my memories of the few times she
felt romance and tenderness.
She always recalled to me that she had
no privacy in her young adult life,
she and her brothers were like a rim of plátanos
hanging tight to each other.
Grandmother died young swinging away the pain

cervical cancer by swaying in her hammock.
Left my mother matriarch of the Hernández tribe.
When she made the New York jump,
they all kept coming, one at a time, to live
near her.
At times after she'd finish cleaning,
a bolero playing, I'd find her crying in a corner.
We did thousands of somersaults to stay
up with the bills.
When the winters brought ice inside the windows,
she would scrape it off early, before my sister
and I woke up.
When sister Gladys was a teenager she found
a job at Eye and Ear hospital
had to get there right after 5:00 a.m.
My mother would always walk those seven
blocks with her cold dark winter mornings, freezing.
I would go with them, the man of the house
since I was eleven. My mother would take
an iron pipe through the dangerous streets.
My mother lived in fear of everything
going wrong.
She lived within that fatalism 'til the end.
Her heart functioned for others—
what belonged to her? Dedication.
You don't see that anymore.
My mother was a light yellow, as upon her
fell the skin of my grandfather's family.
It was her sister Chela that got the African
tinge of Augustina, my grandmother.
Mother's finances and responsibilities

were always in proper order.
Her nerves made her jump with an appetite
that kept her a full, round, heavy mama of the
mountains.
That bacalao with boiled plantains,
cake and Pepsi, a sweetness
so out of control it led to early diabetes.
In fear, she locked herself up the last twenty-
five years of her life. She enclosed herself in a
private cell of illusive bolero lyrics.
It seemed she was always preparing
to reach a point where she could live
and be happy, a place where there was
serenity.
So much pain at the end
that creation intervened and took
this Rosa, May flower, month of her birth,
month of her death.
She told me the stories of the past
when we coffee and bread and cheesed
together slices of sweet guayaba paste, incidents of
people long gone, now in the mountain
forest chirping as birds,
or pressed inside trees of caoba,
voices at night whispering into dream ears.
I took her memory all in,
lucid 'til the end. Little by little
my imagination sees them like a "once
and-now-then," as "once upon a time"
and "two are three."
I felt each hurt with her as she slipped

away.
It's like your birth, your death,
you know nothing, both in the hands of God.
We remain incredulous that such a life
could have been with us, such
sacrifice. Her old calderos, who could
ever have that rhythm of hands and sofrito?
Tough like the Roble tree,
a bickering flower who told the cruel truth.
Tears come out of my fingers
onto the writing pencil and moisten the paper,
which is like the handkerchief she once
dropped by the fountain in the plaza,
and my father picked it up.

Jíbaro Mood

Out of nowhere guava bushels arrive in
the back of my mountain house,
with a dance of lilac flowers waving beside them,
breeze, pollen inspires its own migration.
It's a land that I work from the edge of a book,
many suns now that I don't machete the bush.
Each time I want to get out there
a flurry of words makes a wall in front of me/
the tall grass must be trimmed
my neighbor let loose twenty goats to bite
and chew
giving me time to sway, hammock with volumes,
classics where insects become letters.
A coma suddenly moves across
the tropical Taino zabana of my floating
hammock encompassing my mental maraca bop
be cool limps from ancestral bed.
Someday I will get to the plantains, which
are now thick before they ripen, the
birds will plan a feast. And they will not
invite me.

Inside Caribbean

1
Okra
that slides
with malanga as the bacalao
wet with olive oil
pushes into the yucca
still dry
moving toward
the edge of the plate,
oh, how delicious it is.

2
They are of almonds,
guayabas not,
before the guayaba
almonds raise delight,
white dress. Son slow,
shoe brush, wood floor, piano
changes midair, to remind
they are of almonds,
guayabas not. Strut adjusts,
but for the dizzy who want
to rumba, don't forget,
they are of almonds, guayabas not.

Cartegena de Indias

Caribbean cities share in the humidity,
which hovers the whole sea,
they were the first to see the Spanish ships.
In Colombia I sweated the walk recalling the
architecture of old San Juan,
the Roman pillars, the arabesque archway doors,
all these portals the first settlements of the
buccaneers/thieves
who later claimed respectable daughters
who spoke French and played piano.
Oh look now, I see them coming through
Parque Bolívar, fanning the air around them
to blow away the native voices screaming
in agony-shrills of Indias whom their great-great-
grandfathers violated.
Cannons sticking out into blue vastness,
were poised so as to protect
what had been recently stolen.
What should be said to the natives of Isla Calamari,
that years later they are tourists in their own land.

The pictorial song of the rainbow when
moisture and sun orgasm an arc,
while below the sun sprays gold,
the steeples, the gardens between rain clouds,
incoming charcoal, a rosy magenta above
the Spanish ships, which look like castles

coming in from heaven
as the falling sun obscures the line of the sky.

A month later they leave with twenty thousand
pounds of silver the ship sunken deeper
into the water.

Entering by sea, Cartagena hangs
like a necklace of beads, a
melody of houses, rows of Spanish
beams covered with cement,
windows, narration of history,
loud ship horns as you sip café
in La Plaza de los Coches.
The moon comes down with black hair
splashed with makeup, lips smeared red,
and she will kiss any buccaneer
who gives her a little box
in the shadows of the alleys.

The streets are back in the 1600s
and you are there breathing the legend,
Andalusia entered tropical history,
its shapes and squares,
its sharp swords, the blade
that cuts the nose out of faces
while it breaths the last whiff of saltine air,
silver contraband, a hundred thousand swords
lay at the bottom of the Atlantic.
The Romans are the Latin slash, which is dead
within us.

We walk possible through the streets,
elevated each time we turn a corner,
the theater of Zarzuela,
so far from Madrid. Distant.
The rules change, the Spanish softens,
aligns itself to the sweetness of local fruit.
A voice whispers—is it a song.
The morena beckons from the bushels
outside of the enclosing muros, walled city,
no law existed,
yet inside the walls what law was there,
the law of thieves, the numbers conspired
to their advantage.
All the Caribbean speaks the same meaning
in various languages.
Now they say they *salsa* in Madrid, in Sevilla
in Granada,
what hard stones for families
that now have to suffer the love
of those who destroyed us.
Below the cobblestones the secret chambers of
El Morro,
of the Captains,
they tied brujas and whipped them,
they baked people in the sun.
The Middle Ages linger, did you not
see Trujillo barbwire in Santo Domingo?
The pure Castilian imperialist diluted
their blood, sweetened,
made more beautiful.
We are still standing with our mouths

wide opened in disbelief at what
has happened, a mystery even unto
ourselves.
Cartagena, like time in reverse
the conquest reappears. What exquisiteness,
the yellows and magentas, the sky hugging
ayuntamientos, the old library, the hands
of the fishermen pulling in the ropes and
tying knots. What could it be with the
cumbia by the sea spices closer to Africa
across the liquid glass, sing Petrona, the name
sounds like dynamite, or some chemical,
petron, some acid jumped out of tree smeared with
reptile saliva. When she calls to rhythm,
our feet listen.
In this maraca of the street that rattles,
I am in each somewhere else, seeing the
same rhythms,
in shapes, local
clusters of the white minority still trying to
command.
The street, night, Vallenata,
through the rows of the Martyrs proud stone,
listening to the ocean,
we in front of the Teatro Heredia mouths a-droop.
Nothing has to be happening at the theater,
it is just a splendor to observe
the light hitting the golden windows,
beautiful despite the tragedy of the zarzuela
that plays inside.
Another corner, the sherbet coco is for los locos.

The flavor vanishes between two auburn
houses like mango pulp stuck between
the teeth.
Beaming windows—one spoke to us
as we searched the Caribbean rhythms,
pursuing the violence that made the architectural urban
flower
when New York was nowhere.
Modernism first came to José Martí,
Rubén Dario, echoes in the jungle,
dragging motion of the anacondas.

The past alive in front of us
walking through cafés,
tables outdoors in the air,
wind wave push made the
caffeine impulse think of storms,
bottles of water fell over, spilt onto
beige pants
behind the tables and tiles. A medieval wall,
dirty and spent from so much sunlight
and night saltine air,
lovers dancing with their fingers
they look like people
who might be reading Alejo Carpentier
and Rubén Dario back home,
the poet who once contemplated the sea
in search of Greek sirens
with his eyes of cacao lust.

Stationed outside a window that speaks:
I am window upon this street of time,

cannonballs have missed me,
argument beyond the beauty of my
arabesque curves.
I don't know the noise or the progress
I stare into the vast sea that disappears
eventually into the coast of Cadiz, Spain.
Back home as I am here, opening
shutting while the centuries pass
I have heard flavor made visible,
tomato gazpacho,
the refrains of Pancho Panza,
kingdoms rise and fall,
Cervantes in an Algerian jail,
the jasmine that penetrates
the rose, which becomes liquid,
sprinkled upon the wasted walls
of the Fortaleza (old San Juan)
where the torture dungeons are hidden.
There was a period when
walking bones rattled around the plazas,
houses crumbled as flesh turned into stench,
the masters complained that the slaves died
young,
a man told us, a drinker, that many were maimed,
had burns and hernias, many health problems
the overload of work, such stress under the sun.

The Catholic priest such and such would appear
with auburn curls like steps in his head.
Oh mother the archbishop has arrived from Rome,
how curious, how darling he looks.

We end up by the house of El Gabo
(Gabriel García Márquez)
he is not there, perhaps in Mexico
dining with Álvaro Mutis.
Gustavo tells all this in
that singsong hop of Colombian accent,
that first boulevard right off the sea, the gold sand,
a busy curve of flowing vehicles
public buses look like decorated stages
from bottle caps to bells and dolls hanging
while the Vallenata thumps.
We walk looking up through each of the streets
of swaying balconies.
I am inside of a painting
when our hunger meets history
we eat Africa, with the Mediterranean
smoked with native herbs. Restaurant.
Cobblestone streets
A flute pierces a line through tambor
Vallenata
as we flavor food in a structure that can collapse
at any moment,
but it would rather pause in time.

Bacalao and Society

Was it the Portuguese or the Basques who
first came upon the waters of Terranova
and discovered that vast supply of bacalao
fish jumping in northern sphere waters?
After the saltine pesca did they make
their way to Orchard Beach Bronx?
Back-lac-guise.
Cod, the gold of the ocean.
It was the food of the exploration voyages,
preserved by salt, the origin of *salary*,
coming into bays coasts of lush green
discovered yucca for the tongue.
The Basque went crazy with the
gadus morhua.
New land turf their nets
hooks, action busy, the fish jumped
onto the boats like there was no choice.
The men of Portugal far from the women
of Lisboa hummed songs of sadness.

The fado in the shadows of nocturnal
Lisboa taverns back home
when not traversing the avenues of the sea,
stealing/buying people from Africa,
bring them to Sevilla for Spanish sales,
generations of Walof Yoruba Mandingo Carabali becoming

Catholics-Ladinos church Sundays,
later they left for the new world,
not all in chains but some as conquistadores,
eating bacalao on the ship,
and eventual naked Tainas as well, boca baca.

Bacalao ala Vizcaino, Basques an old
people, Cro-Magnon skulls, don't know
if they fall into the Imazighen Berber sphere,
say whom the Guanches across the
waters from the Tamzight Afriquia sounds, tall blonds
walking the Canary Isles, the beauty of
not knowing, white blonds painted
upon Egyptian murals, all spread across
the northern head of Africa.

The Portuguese found Brazil our neighbors
in bacalao,
Carnivalesque flesh, hey Angola dance,
fado with rhythm, everything that moved
sexed each other, now the people look
like cuisine dish: dry cod with clabaza,
jungle herbs, mountain tubors, yucca, malanga,
ñame, aguascat.
Elaborate wraps of the Catholic ceremony,
the priest like an Egyptian decor, pageantry
that parades carnival,
for weddings or baptisms,
boil cod or saute with tomato Mexicualt,
Mediterranean olives, in every geography
the same moon appears, beams down

zit eyeball of all our memories.
Consider rows of light-blue houses,
balcony where the mestiza cools with a Sevilla
fan in eternal exile,
inside a fire boils the saltiness out of the fish
erasing sodium,
sweet in the raisins, or happens what
local color, what the earth is giving you
from out-of-town mountains vecindad.

Did the sailors stretch out the oars in
search of more bacalao,
imagine new coastal curves, bays of breasts,
nipples?
Settlements where the lust was greatest,
community, children, the dinner table.
For cooking long hours you space time
with songs, which hum within you,
the cod shaky and loose crumbles
at touch of fingers, just out of the hot water,
will split into any shapes of desire,
which the tongue lashes.

The Basques stayed home but the Portuguese
got all parts of the world, left their DNA in the tropics,
and then like an octopus whose tentacles have
touched fire zoomed back home.

How many bodies of cod used to
skinny-dip off Newfoundland,
Terranova encounters, not for the soil

but for the Italian baccalà to squeeze
even the liver for its oil,
memory off of Massachusetts Cape Cod
fishermen's port.

The dish I like most is serenata de bacalao,
like the songs that used to come to balconies
to arouse the interest of a woman
by the troubadour who wants to be
her lover,
such is what memory eats.

Groenburgewal Straat

to Dutch friends Steef Davidson y Gea Stadig

Amsterdam
walking through the canal streets
of cold November, wind and water,
from window observe ducks in caravan
floating gracefully observing the pedestrian
traffic,
staring toward the old houses collapsing
from the weight of the sky.

Such coffee windows, reading Márquez
so far from the Caribbean, enjoying pancake round
cream sweet, inside, turning pages, safe from
the cold, the radiator background sound,
lectura imagining the depth of the water.

The natives had told us
we could get a boat and go out through
the canals, so we did.
We sat while a giant chamber filled
with water to raise us up to the level of the
stream, we left almost losing the boat because
captain forgot to undo the rope that held us to
a steel post. He did wake in time from
blurry hashish waves.

We entered one creamy town after another,
floating in the stream high above the land,
looking down upon the cows, which seemed
like dinosaurs, the street of wooden shoes,
it was another time, just looking at the store signs,
the letters thrown like dice chance
how could the *a* follow an *x* or an *h* by
b, what sounds, what syllables, we could
not enter the speech even less the written
language falling all around us.

We managed to get back to the city level.
Inept captain smiling, he ate too, and drank
fresh keg beer, truly God looks over us.

The colors of Van Gogh call our eyes,
entering the Rysk Museum.
We start smelling food coming from the walls,
bread and fruits, still life with wine,
goose and slabs of beef, Dutch masters
paint succulent, bacchanal feasts.

The guards follow spectators to
make sure they have no forks
or knifes.
It seems a figure in a Rembrandt painting
insulted a passing man—
the man pulled a knife and slashed the
face of the canvas.

Amsterdam is circular, a pancake
streets make hooks loops circles
into each other,
They seem to rotate like an antique
merry-go-round, constantly whole sectors
relocate as when you're lost at night
searching for a hotel that has disappeared.

You find Indonesian jade on the corners
inside gouda cheese Curaçao coconut,
colonialism gives and takes,
energy colonizes the rancid Edam cheese.
The sounds of gongs
announce the appearance down
the canals of ancient Pacific boats,
old booty stored in chests,
invading the memory.

Rotterdam of infinite
bicycles rotating boulevards, abandoned
with no chains or locks in front of
the cafés,
saw a woman of red hair such that it seemed
painted,
closer no pierced ear in her modernity,
that might be for the Latin gypsy peoples,
the African bend of decoration.

Various nights I dreamt with water,
with open sea entering my cup of coffee,
my head sticking out in the center of the Atlantic,

wake up into cold insane furnishings.
Marijuana and teas, herbs all sold together,
herb store, weed classified, Colombian, Mexican, Thai
pay at the cash register, go home with
your herbs,
without thinking about cops.

The moon is a round gouda cheese,
holding back the water of this hollow land,
which lives in fear of baptism.

Petra-Jordan

Are the stones actually the people who once
were Nabataeans?
The city flesh frozen
in stone language—
what sound could that script have been in breath?
An Aramaic that shifted tracks
toward an Arabic destiny.
Petra—stone was the morning of the
Arabic script,
the curves of its letters, the domes of the
cliffs.
What could I have been in piedra Petra
rolling with ceramic hands,
in distant view a Roman chariot.

They channeled the flowing rain water
safely into aqueducts, stored.
As late afternoon darkened to invite the night,
the water shined like blue ink,
the camels moved slowly down the steep
corridors of the mountains loaded with spices
bound for the coast,
sandals strode
cliffs,
which hinted at the rosy color of women's buttocks.

Discovered Petra during the trip I took
to Amman, Jordan.
Entering through the immense gorge, I thought
about the Arab writers I spoke to the day before,
lots of Palestinians, some hostile and indifferent
no matter that I looked like them—
it was a United States–sponsored talk.
Listen brothers of the words,
should we not crush Petra to make
weapons of stones, send them down to Gaza
for the teeny rockers of liberation.
Such is the world that no one sees.
There I am with German tourists, some Italians,
from the side, the people looking
must have said "looks like an Arab walks
among them."
The Nabataeans once chiseled and chiseled
to make homes in the rosy hardness,
which were also tombs waiting for bones.

Amman of the falafel streets,
large neighborhoods of mansions,
light skin black hair sultanas
hidden behind veils,
eyes stepping out like marvelous big marbles
the hijab and nikabe emphasizing ojos what is most
beautiful in women,
at the university room full of shawls
who were poetry, as I held the page,
amazed as their nikabe veils rose and fell

with the moisture of each breath. Petra is the hardest
        place ever,
like where the Flintstones lived.
It was the natives who fashioned the alif,
who gave letters the wings of black birds.
It was the lengua that spread the
Koranic word, crossing oceans and deserts
into the Spanish peninsula, into the grammar,
the vocals of the Hispanic morning.

What spice and perfume once floated
the sandstone cave dwellings
what mats and pillows to soften coitus,
aroma of melted flowers,
winds of Semitic, Greek, Arabic spices
pushing through the hard walls.
What lasts a forever if duration is a thought,
a construct, the earth dwellings free.
Allah is the realtor, a glimpse
of eternity, of afternoon, of fresh blue sky,
mineral houses, below
the falcon's incessant flight,
above the Middle East.

Cantigas of Santa Maria

*I use the same title as a sequence of song/poems written by
Alfonso X el Sabio, to take them to another realm. He was
dizzy at times, half baked at other moments, contradictory.
He adopted Castilian as the official lengua of Spain, giving
the vernacular with all its Arabic words a lift toward
Spanish. Latin had removed itself from the streets and the
taverns. People did not understand it all, except for clerics
and some court people. The Spanish dog now dances in
Colombia, Puerto Rico, Argentina, Patagonia, the end of
the world, and continues until the mambo of our days.*

I sing to Maria. This day on this island
the ones that I know, the one across
the street, the one that I once saw, through
the tropical panorama, the ones who were
in Sevilla and their smiles come to me
through history, the ancestors of my mother,
the ones in the books of Córdoba, the ones
who were also Miriam of the Arabic sounds,
Marias who now walk through valleys,
towns, and plazas of central America.
"Os no la veis."
This Galician verse
full of the ones that King Alfonso x the Wise,
the knowledgeable powdered,

cousins of his Jewish and Muslim musicians
they were water bearers bringing water,
sweetness with sweetness tastes so much sweeter.
To the Marias stuck with evil men,
ill mannered, bad faith ones, cough vile.
Depraved fell on that
thoughtless day for the wild loose horse,
perfumed for the occasion, scent of patchouli,
enough to dizzy anyone, for you must know
awareness takes breaks when most need it,
dangerous, with all the criminals in rampage.
To those Marias my blessings.
My mother said *people are a movie*
she would say, *la gente que si quien los ve*
the people, as if who would see them,
then you realize they are upside down,
pure images in bembe lip, labial brooms,
don't fall asleep at the mouth of a pig
rump boc fume trump porcine shit
if you swoon in it—takes two decades
if you awake,
if you don't it will take you to the fires
described in Dante's *Inferno*, molten, scorched,
red rocks for pillows.
Alfonso El Sabio insisted, so he
became a hole in the moon.

Remember Maria in the stable holding Jesus
against all odds, and Roman vipers she withstood.
Veiled Miriam next to the arabesque marmol
minaret of the Grand Mosque of Córdoba,

the webs of spiral circles, curves, a language
of spiderwebs in the wind, a
repeating chorus melting in her eyes.
O Miriam of one single glance
that now I remember for an eternity.

I sing to the Miriams in this Moroccan land,
zejels of night rhythms that buttock drum stars
dangerous eyes, Andalusia, later the Caribbean.
The jellabas hold down the curves of sight, an
intuition, old ways of saying song,
dancing, delicate weaving in the silk day long,
bones and flesh denote a substance, a cream
invariably one pursues the substance of the dream.
Wake up one day, notice the stream,
the gift of rhyme that Andalusia sent to Europe,
constant gentleman of love refined,
through Arabic poetry of well-measured time.
Taking off her shame in perfect rhyme.
I miss not a girl of those that avenue march—
images for the later night verse,
flying out of the pen in my hands into the sky.
Alfonso's Maria, mother of Jesus,
miracle worker among Muslims and Jews,
reviving horses, separating armies, making
them invisible to each other.
Saving Moorish girls from towers in flames.
What did he see in the canticos he heard from others.
It was a different where and when,
cannot imagine the articulate brutality,
Spain of severed heads and hands.

Teresa de Avila's hand still floats in embalming fluid
in the namesake city of medieval crumbling streets.
In that Spain of slain mentalities,
collective schizophrenia, small-minded operations,
some of it later glossed in Cervantes's *Quixote*.
They were all Sancho Panzas.
The dream of Dulcinea, the quest for the morena—
so beautiful in certain Córdoba paintings—
'til this future Mira Maria, how she walks,
passes by, all the air consumed,
leaves you pale, against a wall, gasping for oxygen.
Hail Miriam, against all the forbidding laws of pleasure,
raise to Eros. Did you not rise to heaven,
flesh bones and hair complete,
to walk upon the original minerals of green gloss.

I sing to the black of her hair,
canto to the flower rose of her lips,
to the guitar of her shape,
to the destiny of her love, flesh and divine.
Mary, Mary the little lamb
wonders within you as the nighttime stars design.
María, Miriam, morena, Mary.
Morena, María.
Bird Mary caramel dancer
Ave Maria morena.

Vicente Espinel–La Decima

*para Isidro Fernandez-Hernandez el Colorao, Trovador de
Aguas Buenas*

I am street Malaga,
exactly breeze of Ronda,
turf of old quarters Arabesque
Architectonic,
the tavern I frequent
so near to her house,
her husband is wood, timber,
but her eyes are fire
and follow my rhymes
each of the times
she passes,
I strum my vihuela against
the door
as she strolls I can feel her
through the floor,
my eyes dance the movement
of her curls
if her husband wants to settle,
what Manolo pendence wants,
I provide the testicular designs,
what the songs spell in the sky,
the birds I just hung my decimas upon,
as they fly from tree to flower.
Minerva you are the ink of my words,

I borrow what is in the
air and belongs to no one,
what the eye peels I violate,
in the future Buñuel will slash
an eyeball,
sign of the screaming image.
Andalusia, sight is rapture.

The song escapes through the breath
of liquor,
Arabic hymns have become Latin.
People speak and almost dance
with the words, making motions
and sounds.

Some nights back the police came,
as I circled with the horns
the bolero jealousy of our knifes,
town hall wants me to pay them
a fine, instead I pay with time,
which is the passage of my body,
divided into syllable of octaves,
my sentence of eight syllables.
Three days and I have more songs
to flower upon the girls,
that divine chance brings into Eye.

Who has escaped with the old moon,
which shines the light of the sun at night,
is it she who knows where my lover has

gone, that's why the wolfs howl at the
disc so bright.

The melodies float taberna,
perfume, which I slice down to the
metrics of my poetic cape,
neatly into my frames,
Minerva her husband somewhere
makes boots of leather,
she is free we dance again,
I measure her exactly,
the fifth string appeared in my lust,
a necessary sound.
The vihuela is my knife
O Manolos, miscreants
come to the feast, eat something
sweet to endulce your life.

The tips of women's fans wave in their
hands secret messages to others,
to their lovers,
desire fills the air escaping from their
dancing hands,
oils perfume circulate,
white teeth, black hair,
bar candle lit we are all shadows
almost ghosts.

Everything is so old
what are we the Arabs, the Moors,
the Greeks, what are we the Romans

the Berbers of such northern rise.
Spread from Andalusia this decimal
of the popular song.
Embraced by the street and the
mountains of the workers,
the ceramic and leather people
take to the taverns to wine and
sing.
The mestizo impulse in Mexico:
"de la sierra morena, cielito lindo, vienen bajando
un par de ojitos negros,
Cielito lindo de contrabando"

Vicente Espinel lived in the early
1600s, despite his university and books
he also roamed the popular street of crooks
and not that he wasn't a priest, surely
he knew the weight of each offence,
he carries his cross through the deformed
wilderness,
the ten-line form was before him
he conceived the rhyme pattern of the decima,
dwelling in taverns with street picaros,
wine and testicles splashed against
the monotony of popular culture
where the lack of everything builds
the anger,
for the bronk is sure to come.

Ronda was in Muslim hands
for the longest time

Almost as much as Granada,
which fell to Christians ten years later.
The reconquest was a civil war
fought by Spaniards of different religions.
The arabesque archways in old Ronda,
the tiles were like Arabic script sprinkled upon the floor,
the troubadours did they still conceal
songs in Moroccan dialect,
that come to the ear of the poet.

Espinel like Cervantes fell into the hands
of Barbary pirates,
spent slave jail time
whistling tunes in Algeria.
The decima still lives in the substrata of the language
paises of Latin America
from Argentina to Mexico
decima singers in Louisiana
descendants of Canary island immigrants.

Just yesterday the trovador Isidro Fernandez
El Colorao de Aguas Buenas
let loose an Ay le lo lay to echo
through the mountains of Caguitas.
I recognized instantly
that he was blurting out
a salutation in Arabic
a salute to the night,
which is *layla* in Arabic
fill in lil lalay
Ay lelo lay praising the night

commencing his song
as our Arabic ancestors did
in al-Andalus.

The Albaicin

The old neighborhood rises like vanilla ice cream
white milk in Granada as in the Lorca poem
where he described milk as white. Lorca called
upon the brightness of the whole. We suppose
all that color is milk, but in case you didn't see it,
white milk, or the lizard that was for
him a drop of a crocodile. This exaggeration,
or concentration
this emphasis is al-Andalus, today Andalusia,
capital of region Sevilla.
Rows of chalk squares rising up
like a row of teeth.
Horseshoe windows, door was curved,
Stained red glass. The streets where Latin
took its shape into Spanish, with the
perfume of Moroccan songs.
The people of the camel, of the horse,
the desert strollers, don't even think
where you are going, just move forward,
there is nothing you are following,
invisible wind is your guide. Lost!
You have this word in your vocabulary?
Danger is if you are found then you
know not where you going, or where you are,
always everywhere lost.
The garden's sudden jasmine scent

Like a whistle kiss, a nymph street walks,
a tree dances, China citrus, some rolling.
Ah the Alhambra in the distance from
this café of canto jondo.
The poet Juan Ramón Jiménez watched as
Buñuel films the sky, captures the horizon
toward the caves of Sacromonte,
where streets curve into mineral parlors,
bedrooms of rock
next to a thousand pots. La Golondrina
sits singing, combing her hair.
The night sits over la Sierra Nevada
before it enters Granada, still and silent,
folded as if in prayer. What duendes
does it hold, what dances, what loves.
The very fingers, which
touch the jewelry, jealous upon the caress
of the knife. It's just that
my whole sky loved her so much
that once I cried like a child,
and she never came to caress,
embrace, left me crying in the night.
Mama where were you?
The tears became glass
cutting my mouth, as the red tears dried
upon my laughing lips,
this picture of Granada
architecture reflected in the serenity
of the water dance frozen mirror
melting with the
Arabs dancing in the windows.

The gypsies came way after the
trovadors were trembling from desire
and sadness. Those Indian feet that
came dancing into the happy/alegre
hurt, so much hurt that humanity
wants no more, hurt or love.
Desire rises in the slums, shantytown
adoration.
In Granada I had to be stopped
from
taking the sword from the side rib
of Jesus, suffering in the mosque
where the invaders left him to die.
Isa of the morning prayer
handing us keys to doors.
Water becomes an orange
talking fish.
Torrential rain of Koranic suras
recitation through the canto deep.
Forgive me Granada
I lament the absence,
forgive me
if I have caused this storm, painted
over the Sierra Nevada of memory.

Sepharad

*to Lawrence Ira Kahn, known in the New York Rican
community as Larry Harlow el Judío Maravilloso, the
Marvelous Jew swinging salsa piano*

When at a certain corner of Córdoba
a cool on the loose cat walked
passed the old Jewish
cemetery the hair of his meow
stood up as if he was hearing
whispers or kabalistic prayers
emanating from the ground,
poised later at the foot
of Maimonides statue
near the Almodovar Wall,
with a stare like he owned all
distance.
I walked toward a café
on Manriquez and Almanzor street
corner where the intersections collided.
The cat had already traversed forward
with his tail like an antenna
gathering wind, Guadalquivir breeze.
I stepped in my cordovan shoes,
leather, the pavement, brush,
found a table while in the middle
seat,
Ibn Gabirol turns the pages of a study,

Ibn Hazm writes half a mile
of prose on a single glance,
a feminine bird flies
with her sight on fire,
if the eyes look up while her
face is lowered, if it is a sideways
glance, it means such and such,
if the eyelashes dance, it
means such and such else.
Periods and commas, commentary
along the way. So much the eyes
talk, behold just a *behold* look,
it is also a sound.
The eyes belong to Anna, to Sonia,
to Sabiya, and Alejandrina.
They pave roads in the night.

Just café con leche I tell the
waiter, I was waiting for
Moises Cordovero as a note arrived
that he was in town from Toledo.
A neighbor who is custodian of the
synagogue on Calle de la Juderia sent it.
It was habit of Yusuf to always drink tea in
this café, with the breeze parallel
to the nose of Ibn Rushd (Averroes).
All the Jews in Hebraic or
Arabic, all the same to them,
right to left upon the blank horizon
as they
mingled with the caliphs and their

families, stayed with them long nights
as doctors they monitored their health.
Maimonides did medicate and prescribed,
just as sure as he is now stoned
by the wall next to the cups of café
aroma.
Wondering about the language
for this celebration, I myself
am within a word in a language
that pulls my coat, as I remember
that my mother is holding my hand,
we are turning a corner on the Lower East Side
Manhattan on our way to Orchard Street—
no trees or Perdes gardens,
a brick ceremony lined in union
to look for clothes, school upon us
in the September of cool awareness.
Orchard Street was like a Middle
Eastern bazaar with prices flexible.
From a distance we hear the
ancient Jews,
the ones who accompanied the Greeks
as merchants into Iberia,
singing the singsong bargains
into the Mediterranean wind.
What is my mother talking about with
my aunt Chela, as we floated
by these caravan faces speaking
cubist Spanish,
almost grabbing them by the arms
dragging them into the stores,

where boys pants and shirts
stacked up to the ceiling.
Are they Sephardim from the old
country that we must all remember,
are they speaking Semitic alligators
pliers turning bolts and screws
in the Latin classic dancing Arabic
syntax laud spilling into the
lengua becoming
aquí se habla español
We are now old vocals
in New New York.
River East flows nearby.
What happened to the cordovan shoes
of my father's walks,
the leather of his skin,
the strut of his horse,
I recall he jumped a propeller
airplane before us.

When we arrived,
my mother accused the apartment
he got for us of having
the smell of a woman, lipstick,
perfume, scent soft upon the walls,
near these metallic things with
rolled-up Jewish prayers.
My mother and Aunt Chela
do not pencil any of these thoughts.
They just make pasteles of green
bananas, arroz and gandules
of Christmas Eve

yucca chopped into mounds.
A drop of my Manishewitz wine
descends upon a slice of avocado,
which is a smile balanced
on top of plantain and yucca
still recuperating from the
rain fall of Goya olive oil.
Mother and Chela
traverse through Orchard Street
in search of specials.
Make that dollah stretch,
mofletched railroad
tenement apartment flat.
Me and this guy Malanga took
to opening these mezuzah metal
boxes, opening up scrolls, the
handwritten prayers in Hebrew stretched
out on our brown palms
dreaming of coconuts.
Poricans painting them pink over
doorways and living room walls,
spot like a Valencia Bakery wedding cake,
tell me Urba if I am in the sason
atop what, what!

We came from a desperate
Caribbean island
weaving what was locked
in the Spanish language,
it was a shawl made of sound.
Where I came from we spoke
tobacco language,

the tongues were made of leafs.
An oral dialect,
our libraries were made of wax,
albums of
Trio Los Condes, Johnny Albino,
Ramito, mountain troubadour
beckoning for layla lo lay night,
for her warm legs.

I stepped into Córdoba again,
through the history of a dream
hidden in a mezuzah, flowing
the Guadalquivir.
Jewish Sufis compared notes
with Muslims, the night is cold
and the rooftops
wake me with their steps
against the sky.
That night the Latin dance hall
had a Marvelous Jew playing
salsa piano, my ears
again buzzing, loud speakers,
the Kosher Son Montuno
of Larry Harlow.
Rhythms in my history,
rhythms colliding
inside one another
poly storm of drums,
Andalusi classic,
Cuban son, Córdoba,

New York flows near River East
the cold wind erasing what
history, the night has made.

Malaga Figs

The embroidery of your kisses bewitched
salty Melagueña,
when I walked its streets thinking of the sweet figs.
Behold, tight white pants should not be allowed.
Some city ordinance should be passed,
otherwise who could live,
stunned, engraved in memory.
The Mexican composer Agustin Lara wrote the song
"La Malagueña" without ever stepping foot in Spain or
    Malaga.
Did he sail his mental frames through the blood rivers
of his mestizo bones.
She had a yellow reddish color tinge,
like a fresh fig fallen off a tree
purplish and curved like a laud.
It must've rolled to Mexico City
near the composer's foot—
he saw it and never was the same.
Why go there to suffer?
Azúcar sweetness in sight
out of reach. Helu the night.

Córdoba, 1155

A warm gentle summer day,
cool this morning, café and almond cookies,
a walk through the gardens of the town.
Visit the library looking for a book
by the Greek writer Socrates,
then upon a bench viewing the
Guadalquivir river enjoying the flow of
thoughts and the music of the stream,
children playing all around me,
someone practices a laud, a gitarra,
it drains through accents of almond and jasmine.
The leather workers are opening
their workshops, the smell of mint tea
hovering above the membrane,
city workers are putting up signs,
information about a poets' gathering
at the library close to the big mosque,
not far the synagogue, hence the cathedral.
Servants are scurrying all over the
Emir's palace, sounds of language,
Latin and Arabic, some Berber dialects,
flavor of Hebrew, all the vocal rhythms
colliding one into the other,
a Tower of Babel, people
of color and vibrancy,
the Almoravids people sometimes darker shades

for they once conquered Ghana, Senegal,
Mali blood within them, other Berbers from the
mountainous Atlas North Africa auburn hair
lighter skin. Every variety flows through
these garden-filled streets. Orange trees line the
boulevards.
Just three nights back, the full moon
seemed to swallow the people,
an upward suction accompanied a
mist of jasmine,
when suddenly late at night it must've been
one o'clock, a new black morning,
a group of gazelle girls walked toward a late
open market with a gentle strut like they
had eternity to get there, so all alone
the three of them in black-and-red jellabas.
I wondered, from my repose,
if the moon would gulp *them* up
into its light borrowed from the sun.
Had to leave the reading bench
for the lamp light was
flickering like end of oil.
Ah my city has grown so much,
endless people, so many foreigners
come to study here in our libraries,
schools, quiet gardens to take notes.
In the tight old Medina area, people like a trail
of ants walking, some of the visitors say it's
bigger than Constantinople.
Welcome to my flower of the East
opened in the sun of the West.

Will the future wonder with me
how history will caress us, which way
will it turn us, will they know that we sat
here for generations, families grew, sons, daughters
wives and husbands with grandfathers and grandmothers
Look at Ibn Rushd and Maimonides strolling
toward the baths. Musa perhaps scrubs the
elder philosopher's body clean. How they
must walk out, sparkling after so much conversation
of Aristotle, of the Greeks of old and of the
Egyptians, all things we must study to be
ourselves in this new spirit of air,
whatever humanity will continue to be.
If you find yourself in the future,
think of me sitting in this lovely garden in Córdoba,
my well-crafted leather sandals hugging
my feet,
facing the River Guadalquivir,
the river flowing, flowing, carrying our spirit
with it 'til the end of times. We are like
decoration in time and space. Even if it corrupts,
coming from such exquisite air, it will still be
elegant like a poetic cadence
under the orange and jasmine trees
of eternal motion, standing still in one beat of
Andalusi music, frozen in your hands.

The Map of Spain

The south border of Spain is below
Marrakesh and north right above
Bordeaux.
You can pierce it when you
Listen to guitar routes
being played by olives,
even if you want to get technical
and want to draw blood,
rioja red through the test tubes,
configures moons of nights,
grapes floating like eyes
hanging in the vineyards.
Afternoon walking dates,
fingers hanging palms,
flamenco hips, shaking
amores, flirt, eyes of sharp
jealousy cut into
Arabic canto jondo voices.

I am everywhere in the moons
of Jupiter covered by your shade.
North African wind that blows
right now. Is it moving the rock
of Tariq, as a woman becomes
the laud shape in front of me? Reverberation,
silk like flesh, which is which?

Swaying falcon that has landed
hungry in search of a pigeon.
Polla; I finger scrolls and compare
the winds, sun falling, salt,
East River stoop. Crepuscular mountain,
tropical orange sky. With the Sale pirates,
coffee of darkness, clouds impulse,
the sugar,
a bone chill smack of Mediterranean
coil drift.
Aware of eyes and hands as always,
not foot nor step, don't sleep
within the populous guise.
Survey on the split second
between a Tito Puente beat,
a hidden sharp Berber curve,
amass hodgepodge of malevolent manners
justifying its error in speech folds
of tongues.
The enslaved repeat themselves.

Borders
cannot contain anything,
alien sounds respect no walls
illegal through the ether.
Fluid people are on the dance floor.
Lines spilling where steps measure
chance ambition
disfiguring geography. I am who I
say I am not.
I am who I imagine, dream

each day a different mark.
Identity is a dance of possibility.

Not eye to sea
creatures wet deep
who-isms.
Connected through
my head to a turban, a
Cuban woman, Carlotta,
saw him once,
I hear the breeze that
always shadows me.
Follow lines, little
flickering wings,
motion, animal, the obvious.
What it is, rising
I could only wonder about the
molecules and the atoms
and all the impossibility
that holds it up. How
did so much haziness
become so sharp in
a North African glimpse
spread under a Sevilla olive
tree. The lost Andalus
Cat.

COLOPHON

In the Shadow of Al-Andalus was designed at Coffee House Press,
in the historic Grain Belt Brewery's Bottling House near downtown
Minneapolis. The text is set in Iowan Old Style with
poem titles in Catull Bold.

FUNDER ACKNOWLEDGMENT

Coffee House Press is an independent nonprofit literary publisher. Our books are made possible through the generous support of grants and gifts from many foundations, corporate giving programs, state and federal support, and through donations from individuals who believe in the transformational power of literature. Coffee House Press receives major operating support from the Bush Foundation, the McKnight Foundation, from Target, and from the Minnesota State Arts Board, through an appropriation from the Minnesota State Legislature and from the National Endowment for the Arts. Coffee House also receives support from: three anonymous donors; Elmer L. and Eleanor J. Andersen Foundation; Around Town Literary Media Guides; Patricia Beithon; Bill Berkson; the James L. and Nancy J. Bildner Foundation; the E. Thomas Binger and Rebecca Rand Fund of the Minneapolis Foundation; the Patrick and Aimee Butler Family Foundation; the Buuck Family Foundation; Ruth and Bruce Dayton; Dorsey & Whitney, LLP; Mary Ebert and Paul Stembler; Fredrikson & Byron, P.A.; Sally French; Jennifer Haugh; Anselm Hollo and Jane Dalrymple-Hollo; Jeffrey Hom; Stephen and Isabel Keating; the Kenneth Koch Literary Estate; the Lenfestey Family Foundation; Ethan J. Litman; Mary McDermid; Sjur Midness and Briar Andresen; the Rehael Fund of the Minneapolis Foundation; Deborah Reynolds; Schwegman, Lundberg & Woessner, P.A.; John Sjoberg; David Smith; Mary Strand and Tom Fraser; Jeffrey Sugerman; Patricia Tilton; the Archie D. & Bertha H. Walker Foundation; Stu Wilson and Mel Barker; the Woessner Freeman Family Foundation; and many other generous individual donors.

NATIONAL ENDOWMENT FOR THE ARTS

This activity is made possible in part by a grant from the Minnesota State Arts Board, through an appropriation by the Minnesota State Legislature and a grant from the National Endowment for the Arts. MINNESOTA STATE ARTS BOARD

TARGET.

To you and our many readers across the country,
we send our thanks for your continuing support.

Good books are brewing at www.coffeehousepress.org